Come to the Lights

Chika Agbayi

Frankmond Books—Richmond, TX
Paperback ISBN: 979-8-9910628-0-0
eBook ISBN: 979-8-9910628-1-7
Library of Congress Control Number: 2024913815
Title: *Come to the Lights*
Author: Chika Agbayi
Digital distribution | 2024
Paperback | 2024

Published in the United States by New Book Authors Publishing

Dedication

To my late father—Edmund,

To my mother—Francisca,

Thank you for giving me another chance to fulfill destiny.

Table of Contents

"Caught within the radiant ether amidst the immortals, shall you,
yourself become a god."
— Apollonius of Tyana

Section One
The Awakening

At the Feet of Stillness

Chaos staggers like a drunken soldier,
The voice of Madness floods the night's darkness.
Monotony destroys my interest in life,
Vanity's grip is firm on my soul.
The wind of anger threatens my sanity's flame.
And the wings of darkness root out the light.

My thirst for inner peace shall be my strength,
May the light of love alight my path.
Destroy my worries and drown my sorrows.
Like a lady in her lover's arms,
I shall find peace at the feet of Stillness.

Awaken My Spirit

Sorrows surround my soul
Like enemies surround a man,
Sanity sets on my world
Like the sun sets on dusk,
Madness rises like the Prince of Evil,
Confusion abounds, peace dies in me.

Awaken my spirit and strengthen my soul!

Stir me, Dear Father,
Kill these sorrows, adorn me with sanity.
Fortify my spirit with a sword of light,
And I shall strike down the dark.

Awaken my spirit and strengthen my soul!

Embolden me with wisdom and fearlessness
And ignorant shall be brought to her knees.

Awaken my spirit and strengthen my soul.

On the Verge of Life

Tribulation tries to strangulate peace,
Hate rushes out to drown my joy
Discordant stares and smiles at my world.

My shoulders heavier, my feet blistered,
My sanity wanes, my drive weakens,
Friendly thoughts die save despair.

I sit on the verge of a trembling life
Waiting for Your tall white bliss
To resuscitate my dying world.

Arise

Arise O! Arise within me
And kill the chaos that screams in me.
Abolish the fire of mundane desires,
Cripple my undying lust.
Scatter my hate and anger
Like a gale uprooting trees,
Breaking branches.

Arise O! Arise within me
Let darkness know no peace
And let your light arise like a warrior.
May Your sweet presence cleanse my inner temple,
Let Your light flood it as it rises within.
Your dazzling presence is now in charge,
Peace overflows within.
Arise!

Section Two
On Joy

I Belong to You

I belong to You
Like light to its day,
And the shadow to its owner.
Cleanse this temple within me
Like the dew does to the dawn.
Banish my foolishness
Like the sun does to the dark.
Teach me Your ways
Like a father does to his son.
Stir my soul with deep wisdom
And I shall unleash Your teachings upon the world.

On the Path of Joy

My soul is set on the path of joy.
Misery was slaughtered by happiness,
Anger died waging a war against love,
Discordant drowned on a tranquil sea,
Deceit was blinded in the light of truth.
Is there no reason to rejoice?

My tears of agony turned into joy,
The raging gale broke the wings of deadly memories,
Worries were set on fire, sadness died a sudden death.
Is there no reason to rejoice?

Happiness chanted songs of victory.
Pillars of lights spoke of justice,
A naked wind met a virgin silence
On the bare lawn of shining stars.
I am set on the path of joy.

II

The rain begins to sing a heavenly song,
The night is removing its dark hat.
The moon's beam falls on sleeping souls,
My burden dies in its sleep.

Showers of lights unveil the dawn
A white love wakes me from my slumber,
Such is the way I begin my day.

Once more, I am set on the path of joy.

III

I made few friends on the path of joy.
Brilliance, a tall beautiful lady,
As young as the dawn could be
Lent me her light of beauty.

Love is the immortal warrior of peace
Who shields me from every evil.

Kindness teaches me her ways.
Wisdom, a man of few words
Offers to be my company.

I am still set on the path of joy!

IV

Wisdom raises his voice
Like a minstrel on a lonely road
And speaks thus,
"Life is a master, Time a healer.
Life and Time shall die with earth,
The path of joy is ever eternal.
It is the path of worship, the path of God.
It is like a long tiny road of dazzling lights
Leading to the immortal Heavens of God."
Wisdom smiles and departs,
Silence returns as I walk on.

I remain still on the path of joy!

V

I stand on this narrow road of radiant lights
Where flawless powers travel
On this mystical highway of timelessness.

Joy breaks every barricade and rushes out
Like freedom racing down from a great mountain.
I set aside my fears and self-restraint
To follow this path flooded by joy, by power and by light.

The path of joy is truly the path of worship,
Still I am, on this path of joy.

Is there no reason to rejoice?!

Bliss

Bliss sails my soul
On the sea of intoxicating brightness,
I cease to restrain, choose to let go.

O! Sea of intoxicating brightness,
Sail my soul on the boat of bliss,
To the shore of forever.

The immortal walls of love lies ahead,
Within these walls my soul shall reside
Forever, forever and forever.

A Sword of Light

A ray of the supreme light lies in me,
I wield it like a warrior with a magic sword,
Darkness shrinks, further I advance.

I stand firm on the celestial path of glory
A warrior of light, a warrior of truth,
A defender of humanity, a defender of life,
A bearer of peace for generations to come.

The wind of war roars, my sword shines brighter
Through a blizzard of blitz, I emerge stronger.
Enemies of truth tremble, hate preachers hide,
Lovers of vanity vanish, lovers of lust
Peep from behind the veil of pretense.

Honesty is my shield, supreme light my sword,
Courage floods my path, the battle field is mine.
The king of Illusion rules this place,
I head beyond the borders of earth.
A shinning ship of death awaits,
My battle will soon be over.

Chains of Gold

I gather a lot of gold
 To make a gorgeous home
 Full of roses, milk and honey.
I fly round the world
Like the moon round the earth.

Humanity hails me.
Minstrels make songs for me.
History will remember me.
The staring stars jealous me.

Aha! The weight of my gold
Is too heavy on my soul,
My soul wails out of weariness
Like a burning soul in Hell.

These gold and silver have chained my soul,
I drag these chains everywhere I go,
Like a prisoner of vanity
Dragging the chains of shamelessness
To the Alter of Eternal Madness.

I seek divine hands to unchain my soul
From the chains of mortal desires and lust,
From the strong hands of vanity's grip,
From the paws of this wicked greed.

 I seek the hands that bear the lamp of sanctity
To come free my soul from its deadly slave,
Before the weightless wings of death sail me home.
Let not posterity point at my grave and say:
"There was buried a man,

Whose gold sing a song that soothes the flesh,
  But never the soul."

15

Footprints of Faith

In the dark dungeon of depression,
You approach with hands full of dreams.

From the verge of utter insanity,
You lead me into a charming field of solace.

My heart lacks joy, my spirit strength,
You break the damn of happiness, armed me with vigor.

You refill my cup with the wine of love
My soul forgets the taste of hate.

The sounds of discord disturb my soul,
You lead me into a harmonious realm.

Pain sets on the shores of my mind
Like the sun on the ethers,
Bliss rises like a fresh dawn of blue love.

The hands of hope lead my worries astray.
Shinning dreams stream into my nights,
I rise and brace my soul
To follow the foot prints of faith.

The Hearts of Men

On life's lonely road,
I meet a young amiable lady
Whose language is harmony,
Whose age eternal youthfulness.

Like her majesty's,
Her blue gown of aloneness flows freely.
I stare back at the eyes of compassion,
A soft smile parts her lips.

Without armament,
Agape does her battle in the hearts of men.
She devours hate
Like the inferno does a city,
Cuddles the innocent,
Like a mother does her child.
Her beauty disarms, her grace charms.
She softens the strongest hearts,
Belittles the greatest wisdom,
Crushes the strongest power.
Her courage fierce, her sympathy deep,
She governs all, none governs her.

Her milky lips kiss mine,
Without a word she conquers my heart
And sets out to conquer the hearts of men.

All Is Well

Like a lover deserted by his beloved
Happiness departs my heart.

Like dark clouds gather in the sky
Sadness gathers in my soul.

Troubles conspire against me
Like the wicked against the innocent.

My courage fades, my strength weakens.

My resolve unmoved
Even by the hands of a rushing wind.

Like splinters of stars falling off the sky
Your light suddenly bursts upon my path.

A deep voice rises and says,
"Rejoice, my son. For all is well"

Dreamland

Take me to the land of dreams,
  The land of wonders.

Show me the ancient temples in fairy tales,
Lie beside me and dream with me.

Show me the Land of Wisdom
Where the souls of sages live.

This land is real, life an illusion.
I shall dwell here and never to return.

The Heart of Humanity

L ife is fleeting,
Not divine truth, love and light.

The moment of truth is transitory,
Truth itself survives the stormy weather of doubt.

The scene of love lasts but a while,
Still in the heart it seems like a life time.

The vision of light fades with the wind,
In my heart it survives the raging dark.

I keep my truth, love and light in your heart,
Let the All-Seeing Eye watch over them.

If this heart of Humanity guides my treasures,
The earth will know no lies, hate, darkness nor wars.

Section Three
Supplications

River of Words

From the rivers of words
   I sent forth my devotions to You.
   Let my devotions lie before You
Like a slave before his master.

Accept my devotions,
Let them stir Your spirit
And unleash Your mysterious splendor.
May You roar like the sky roars
With the sounds of thunder.
Alight the entire earth
Like a shining noon with a thousand suns.

May Your beauty awaken the hearts of men,
Cloth the awakened hearts with joy
May the clothed hearts never know hate.
Plant Your seeds of mercy in every soul.
Water the planted seeds with abundant love.
May these seeds grow and kill our hate,
Humanity will rise and find its true home.

I See Your Face

I see Your face in the crying heart of a helpless mother,
In the lonely tears of a hungry child
And in the agonizing thought of a tattered beggar.

I see Your face in the stillness of the wind,
In the darkness sprinkled upon the earth.
I see You smile in the timeless silence of the night.
As the dawn rises, your face still smiles.

The smile I see speaks of greed and vanity,
These twin brothers keep humanity's hearts
Perpetually apart.

Prayer to Freedom

May your will be done oh! Freedom.
The burden I carry is as heavy as grief.
The burden I carry is that of ignorance,
It melts my joy like the sun melts the snow.

May your will be done oh! Freedom.

I sit beside a freezing silence,
Under the tree of patience
Hoping you save humanity from the hands of hate.

May your will be done oh! Freedom.

The night wraps the daylight with the leaves of darkness.
I approach the alter of Your Supreme Conscience,
Weeping for the dying soul of humanity
Led into the vault of destruction by War, envy and hate.
May your will be done oh! Freedom.

The fangs of war is deeply buried in humanity's soul,
Greed feeds on his flesh like vultures on cadavers.

Arise oh! Freedom.

Rekindle the fire of brotherhood,
Awaken the spirit of oneness.
Lead us into this sparkling future I see,
Where I shall love my brother
Regardless of the tongue he speaks,
Where bothers nor boundaries
Shall cease to rise,

Where peace sits on a Mighty Throne
Built on the foundation of kindness.

Before your feet dear Freedom,
We lay our swords, guns and bombs.

A Bag of Fresh Thoughts

The source of all purity,
The creator of joy, the giver of happiness
Who resides in the Ultimate Throne of Heaven.
Saintly souls illuminate Your Throne.
I call You the King of Lights.

I sit in a quiet wood
Listening to the monologue of the wind,
The conversations of the birds,
Waiting for my friend the sun to say goodbye.
Like a youth intoxicated with the wine of life,
My thought goes on a rampage.

With all Your mystical brilliance and celestial glories,
You let vanity destroy man on the vacant field of sorrow.
Pain preys on man, sadness sucks his blood.
Each time he reaches out for survival,
The darkness of depression floods his path.
Each time he wants to rise like courage,
The chain of cowardice pulls him down.
Each time honesty stirs his spirit to think of You,
Lust buries his thought in a woman's thighs.
Each time oh! Each time . . .
Each time true love calls his name,
Hate draws him closer to her bosom.
Why let these happen to Your image and likeness?

My friend the sun says good bye.
I sigh an empty sigh,
The sound of the sigh walks into the wind
The wind walks away, stillness comes.

My thought seems placid.
Evening approaches, I prepare to depart.
Tomorrow will come with a bag of fresh thoughts.

Section Four
The Quest

The Light of Desire

I search for You with the light of desire,
Like a beggar searches for his lost alms with a deathless desire.
I leave humanity for the gentle woods,
Where the wind searches for You in silence too.

My reflections seek for You too
Like the mind of an old poet,
Searching for a long-lost word
In the great sea of deep thought.

Everything mundane is meaningless,
The path of vanity leads to nothingness.
The souls of men are griped by greed,
Whose gown of darkness colors their deeds.

Let the light of my desire rise in search of You
Beyond the boundaries of earthly life,
Let it outshine the colors of death.
Let the light of my desire answer
When Your showers of divine lights call.

Of Thee Alone

I wander from country to country,
From master to master,
From religion to religion,
From the noisy path of prayer,
To the silent road of meditation,
In search of Thee, of Thee alone.

I see nothing but a thick darkness.
My efforts die, my devotions scatter,
Hope flees like a prodigal son.
Courage melts, despair rises,
I search of Thee, of Thee alone.

Let my tears and disappointments
Herald the pain in my heart,
Let prayers and meditations
Herald my thirst for Thee,
Let my thought and my quest
Herald how much I desire Thee,
Let my weary heart and blistered feet
Herald how far I go for Thee, and of Thee alone.

When my days lie breathless
My soul awakens on the other side,
Full of verve, full of power,
Full of love, full of kindness,
Full of light, full of wisdom,
I shall follow the light,
Till I find Thee and Thee alone!

Before the Absolute

I sit in the midst of pure silences
Meditating before Its ever presence,
Protected in the arms of love
I know It stares from above.

Before the Absolute Truth
My innocence stands like a child,
My prayers go on bended knees,
My conscience stripes naked,
My thought prostrates like a slave,
Divine love murders jealousy,
Peace chains my pain.

The Supreme Light alights my soul,
My soul alights the dark.

O! Before the Absolute,
Before that presence that comforts,
My soul is made whole again.

Passion

Like every pore on a leaf
Is filled with passion to worship the sun,
Every pore on my flesh
Is filled with passion to worship Thee.

My life is no longer mine,
I lay it happily before Thy feet,
Like a beggar before his king.

The body is battered, the soul bruised,
My passion for Thee burns brighter.

Atop the mountain on a snowy day,
I feel nothing but Thy presence.

Deep in the valley the river shines dark,
I feel nothing but Thy presence.

On the verge of a trembling life,
Where disappointment chains every door
I feel nothing but thy presence.

In the tenacious paws of poverty,
I feel nothing but Thy presence.

On the long table of riches,
I feel nothing but thy presence.

My life is no longer mine,
The Absolute Truth is now in charge.

My passion for Thee is like a youthful sun.

Purity

Enlighten my fearful soul,
Tear the veil of timidity apart.
Slaughter my fears,
Set my lust on fire.
Let my restlessness be drowned
In the great placid sea of peace.

Let Your light of wisdom rush out
Like a youth intoxicated with the fresh wine of life.
Arouse my desire for Thee,
To seek Thy love, Thy light,
Thy companionship, Thy compassion,
Dear Father.
Like the snow cloths the earth,
Cloth me in purity.

The Teachings

Teach me in Thy temple of solace
Where I face Thy presence without fear.
Teach me to seek Thy face
On every man's on the street of life.

In Thy image, man is made,
On his face, Thine is found.
Teach me about Thy powers
That flow like a golden waterfall,
Teach me about Thy love
That alights the entire earth and beyond.

Like a father leads his child,
Let these teachings lead me
Into the deepest side of solitude.

Here O! Father,
I shall commune with Thee, eternally.

The Higher Power

From the white forest of innocence
Into the colored desert of knowledge,
From the glittering pages of history
Into the misty road of religion,
I wondered in search of Thee.

A sudden abundance of brilliance
Made still my search.
The Higher Power I sought
Was sealed within me
Waiting for a crack,
Just waiting for a tiny crack—on the head!

Seek No Further

Like a mystic I meditate
In soft silences.
Like spirit I dwell in the void,
In nothingness.

A profound peace slains mayhem,
The silvery wings of my soul unfold.
Within me, I commune with Thee.

In my inner vision
The infinite sea of light lies,
The sound of divinity breaks-free.

Within lies the light I seek,
I seek no further.

Immortal Touch

I place not my mind upon my wealth,
For wealth itself is nothing but vain.

I place not my mind upon world's fame,
For fame itself comes with its own pain.

All I acquire is so mundane,
When I die even foes may gain.

Earthly gold make many men slain,
But I have made my path so plain.

I shall follow Thee even in the rain,
If Thy immortal touch is all I gain,
I did not live my life in vain.

Section Five
Eternal Truth

The Sweet Absolute

The Heaven I saw had no angels in it,
Only a blue river of pure love flowing silently,
Flowing, flowing and just flowing
Into its own eternal source that never runs dry.

What a tender river of pure love,
Silently flowing between the banks of purity!

What a beauty to behold!

Happiness summoned tears into my eyes
As I stared at this amazing sight.

Every tear I shed was a drop of joy unimaginable,
This must be God—The Sweet Absolute.

Invocations

I invoke Thee
In my inner temple
Where sanctity sits still,
Where love shines brighter than the sun,
And where holiness is dressed in dazzling white.

I invoke Thee
Where the lawn is made of harmony,
Where the wind walks beside a smooth silence,
And where happiness attends the procession of joy.

I invoke Thee.

I Think of Thee

Tribulations reach out to grasp my soul
The grip of sorrow grows stronger,
I think of Thee.

The light bows out, darkness rises,
Hate rampages, anger goes wild,
I think of Thee.

Greed and lust
Bring war wind to my weak soul,
I think of Thee.

Dreams got burnt, despair abound.
I think of Thee.

I stand on a shaky ground.
Unseen enemies gather around,
I think of Thee.
I think of Thee
And I shall eternally think of Thee.

Undying Stars

On a neutral plane
Where happiness nor sadness,
Light nor darkness,
Sanity nor madness exists,
I devote my thought to Thee
And to Thee alone.

On the state of utter bliss,
The iron fingers of envy
And the bare teeth of rage
Are far beneath my soul,
I surrender my soul to Thee,
To Thee alone.

In the deep spiritual state
The freedom seen by soul is inconceivable,
I think of Home—Eternity,

Where souls sing songs
That shine like undying stars.

Sacrosanct

Under the shade of the tree of thought
I ask the sober wind
To pass my devotions to Thee.

The wind returns with words of joy,
I call the lone birds to share with me
The words of joy, the wisdom of the wind,
The kindness of a Father
And the blessings He showers.

I call upon humanity to think of Thee
Where the wind and the silence
Share the same holy road to joy,
Where darkness ceases to fight the light,
Where souls unite in utter reflection.

This is the sacrosanct place
Beyond the reach of all, but Thee.

A Path of Mystery

Enfolded by the white wings
Of Thy tender presence,
My soul genuflects
And sheds the tears of joy.

My timid arms reach out for embrace,
They meet only the void.
My trembling voice rushes out to sing,
Who dares sing for Thee without great words!?

I doubt if my thought is worthy a place
To think of Thy infinite existence,
Who dares follow Thy foot prints
Without the guidance of purity in white?!

An Ocean of Light

If love is light
And light an ocean,
Let it be massive.

May this ocean of light drown me.
If oceans are bottomless,
May I keep drowning.

Life after life,
Death after death,
Drown me o! deep ocean of divine lights.

The Fruit of the Sun

You are the light that brightens my path,
You are the sword I wield with might
You are the shield I carry with pride.

I am nothing but a mere seeker,
A seeker of truth,
A seeker of light,
A seeker of love.

Truth shines into light,
Light into love,
Love upon the world.

Truth is deeply rooted in love.
Watered by divine light,
It blooms and eternally shines
Like the fruit of the sun.

You are the light that brightens my path,
You are the sword I wield with might
You are the shield I carry with pride.

I am still nothing but a mere seeker of light,
A seeker of truth and a seeker of love.

Brave

Before the feet of Your invisible throne,
He quietly unburdens his heavy soul.

Brave is the seeker of truth,
Brave must be the warrior of light.

With inconceivable brilliance,
You appear before the seeker's sight.

Brave is the seeker of truth,
Brave must be the warrior of light.

Before this inconceivable brilliance that shines,
The seeker remains humble yet resolute.

Brave is the seeker of truth,
Brave must be the warrior of light.

Drowned in this white brilliance,
He casts his life like nothingness before Your feet.

Brave is the seeker of truth,
Brave must be the warrior of light.

His faith strengthens, his will an iron
His love overflows, his passion burns wild.

Brave is the seeker of truth,
Brave must be the warrior of light.

Arm the seeker with words of deep truths,
He shall follow Your will beyond the death of time.

Brave is the seeker of truth,
And brave must be the warrior of light.

What Men Call You

Men call You He or She,
You are neither none of these.

From the minute the earth was made,
Men set out in search of You.

Sages walked the earth and beyond,
Searching for You with mere wisdom.

Mystics went to the mountain peaks,
Nothing was found but an open sky.

Men call You He or She,
You are neither none of these.

To a true seeker You revealed Yourself,
Flooding every path with divine light.

Men call You He or She,
You are neither none of these.

The seeker saw that light within,
And it outshined all else without.

Men call You He or She,
You are neither none of these.

The Nameless One

I call It 'Nameless'
For It dwells in nothingness.

It is beginningless and endless
Still but lives, roars but calm,
Shallow but deep, shapeless but collected,
Luminous but shines not.

All things dwell in It, yet It dwells in nothingness,
All else is fleeting, only It perpetual.
Call It what you will,
I call It 'The Nameless One.'

Nothing

I am endless like a flowing river,
Deathless like soul, older than earth,
Still as the rocks and calm as the lakes.

I am darker than the night, brighter than the sun,
Deeper than the ocean, wider than the sky.

The wise know life is fleeting
And adore me for I am Eternity.

Blistered, bruised, weak, weary
They worship me for I am Eternity.

I am nothing but I am All,
I am All, yet nothing.

I own no fixed abode,
I dwell in nothingness.

I am endless like a flowing river,
Deathless like soul, older than earth,
Still as the rocks and calm as the lakes.

I am darker than the night, brighter than the sun,
Deeper than the ocean, wider than the sky,
Yet I am nothing.

Section Six
The Exit

Images of Death

They say the angel of death
Walks in the dark, ruled by demons,
Gowned in grief, armed with pain,
Shrinks from the light, to invade lives.

I say death is as just as life.
Life traps souls, death frees them,
Both of them are God's angels
Dressed in white by the dictates of the light.

The Foolishness of Men

Before my remains,
Foes rejoice for my earthly death.

Above them I stand,
My soul smiles at their foolishness.

A White Infinite Sea I

Every day comes the same old sun,
Every night a fading moon's beam.
Today knows what tomorrow has in mind,
Every day seems still, steadfast and same.

Young ideas vacate thirsty thought
Eyes yearn to see a different world,
Devoid of the wind of hate and the fire of anger,
The drive to see a white infinite sea awakens.

I now exist against my will.

A White Infinite Sea II

Behind these iron gates of earth
Awaits a soft forever,
Where happy souls dance
To the eternal song of bliss.

Timelessness walks hand in hand
With a disarming beauty.
Ageless roses cushion every step
On this shore of the White infinite Sea of joy.

This is the Heaven I wish to see
When I'm born into eternity.

About the Author

As a teenager, Nigerian born Chika C Agbayi gained a place at Enugu State University of Science and Technology to study law. In 2004, he graduated from the university with an LL.B (Bachelor of Laws) and proceeded to the Nigerian Law School, Abuja, where he got his B.L (Barrister at Law) in 2007 and was subsequently called to the Nigerian Bar. After the compulsory one-year service to the nation, he left Nigeria for the United Kingdom where he studied for a few years. He holds a Master's degree in Business Administration from Heriot-Watt University, Scotland, United Kingdom. His poetries have appeared on ANA Review 2016—A Journal of the Association of Nigerian Authors volume 4. He lives and works in the United States of America.